ACCOMPLISH ANYTHING

SURPRISING

SHORTCUTS TO

SUCCESS

ACCOMPLISH ANYTHING

ANDREW RINEHART

TATE PUBLISHING
AND **ENTERPRISES**, LLC

Published by Tate Publishing & Enterprises, LLC
127 E. Trade Center Terrace | Mustang, Oklahoma 73064 USA
1.888.361.9473 | www.tatepublishing.com

Tate Publishing is committed to excellence in the publishing industry. The company reflects the philosophy established by the founders, based on Psalm 68:11,
"The Lord gave the word and great was the company of those who published it."

Book design copyright © 2012 by Tate Publishing, LLC. All rights reserved.
Cover design by Kristen Verser
Interior design by Christina Hicks

Published in the United States of America

ISBN: 978-1-62024-714-3
1. Self-help
2. Motivational
12.05.10

TABLE OF CONTENTS

WHY YOU NEED TO READ THIS BOOK

I want to be frank.

Accomplishing your dreams doesn't have to be so hard; it doesn't take twenty, ten, or even five years. It doesn't matter where you are right now or where you've been in the past. This is your new beginning. There is a pattern, and more importantly, a system to success. But this is a new kind of success. It isn't what your parents, professors, neighbors or friends have been teaching you and it isn't God given to only a few special individuals. That's right; anyone can achieve it, including you.

My day to day activities, the businesses I run and the people I surround myself with, they all have one thing in common—I choose them. This book is as much about freedom as it is about answering that eternal question of what really separates you from the super-successful. I've managed to make great money in nearly every business venture I've been involved with and I've enjoyed massive amounts of freedom during and as a result of those businesses. I did it as a teenager while living in my parents' basement, I did it as a college student, I did it as a young man in my 20's and continue to do it today, at the age of 28. My life completely changed when as a teenager, I realized that through small changes to behavior and technique, anyone can shape and mold the results of any task, project, sport, hobby or business. With the exception of just a few, you have complete power over the results of nearly every activity you choose to engage in.

The next time someone says, "I want to earn a six-figure income," you'll be thinking in terms of monthly while they're thinking in terms of yearly. The next time someone tells you that you can't become a world class athlete without years of practice and coaching, you'll simply realize that they haven't implemented the Accomplish Anything methods.

Feel free to read this book in the order of the chapters as they are or skip ahead and vice versa. Some of the chapters are in order, others are not. All are stepping stones towards living the life you always knew you deserved.

Your views on business, wealth, entrepreneurship, and life are about to change. Accomplish Anything is your new beginning. Starting right now, your world turns upside down.

MY STORY

My story begins at the age of fourteen. I wasn't the smartest kid, nor did I have the richest parents. I did, however, think about why things happened more than the average teenager. I realized early on that there were basically two people in the world: those that could do (and did) virtually whatever they wanted; and those that were constantly saying things like, "I can't afford it," or, "maybe next paycheck".

Essentially, there were people that said yes, and there were people that wanted to say yes, but were too financially strapped. The latter seemed like a loss of control to me, I didn't want that life. I wanted to be the former, and was determined to do whatever it took to get there. After all, if we aren't in control of our own lives, who is?

So, at the ambitious age of fourteen, I started an importing business. I specialized in clothing and accessories. I purchased sunglasses, watches, ties and other accessories in bulk from all over the world. I brought them back to my hometown in Utah and resold them to a large amount of people throughout the state. Business was booming. I was too young to drive a car during those days, so I would catch the red eye to JFK, spend 6 hours in cabs and subway trains, jump from one dealer to the next and purchase the inventory I needed. I'd be back on a flight to Utah that night. Monetarily, it was an excellent business. I made more money as a 14-16 year old than most of my friends parents did. I was, at that age, able to do and buy anything that I wanted.

At the age of 16, I discovered (to my surprise) that I was running a very legitimate business. I had multiple locations, six employees, and a wide customer base. But even though things were great, I realized that I would never become wealthy in this business. I needed something more. I shut my company down immediately without thinking twice.

My next and more serious venture was...well I had no idea.

I was just entering high school, and even though I was an avid golf and basketball player, my real passion was business. I craved it, I wanted it. I'm not entirely sure where that passion came from but I wanted it so bad it hurt. I knew getting a job or mowing lawns like my friends did wasn't the way to go. If I could figure out how to become a real business owner with a product that had mass appeal, and do it at a young age, I'd have virtually no competition from my peers. After all, most of the kids my age were too busy playing video games.

While on a lunch break during my sophomore year in high school, I wandered into a cell phone store. I told the man at the desk that I could sell water to an ocean. I told him that I wouldn't expect an hourly wage or salary, but simply a flat commission for each phone I sold if he hired me. If I didn't bring him business in 48 hours, he could fire me. Either way; he wouldn't be out a dime in giving me a chance. He reluctantly agreed.

I was to make a $200 flat commission for each phone sold. I left excited, but had absolutely no idea how I would sell wireless phones when, at the time, they were still quite expensive. I called a few of my wealthier friends and ended up selling nine phones in one day—$1,800 profit for a total of 4 hours' work. "Not too bad" I thought, I may be on to something.

Eventually, I became the owner of my own cell phone store. One store grew to two, then a third, and soon I had almost two hundred stores across the country. I built one of the largest wireless phone-dealer companies in the country. At one point, we were opening a new store every day. I grossed just under $100 million in 2007 and traveled the world while I did it, all while still in my mid 20's. I even relocated to South America for over two years. I sold the company a short time later, at age twenty-five, and decided to take some time off.

Being idle bored me greatly. I re-entered the business world shortly thereafter and started several more businesses in the years following, many of which we'll talk about in this book. I have retired at least one additional time to date. I've never had a business that has failed and never had a business that lost money. I've never been an employee, never made a resume, never been through an interview, and never had a job. I sure did create a lot of them, though.

My plans are to run more businesses and retire at least ten more times throughout the process. I have experienced everything that a billionaire experiences, even though I am not one. I purchased my dream home at the age of twenty-four, not because it was for sale, but because I knocked on the owner's door one day and made him an offer he couldn't refuse. Why would my selection of homes be narrowed to just the ones for sale? A limited world is not the one I want to live in. That's how the majority of the world thinks but from now on, it isn't how you and I think.

There was only one thing that set me apart from nearly every other person trying to make it big. It wasn't a higher IQ, financial help from my parents, a better education, or more experience. I simply discovered that human beings have the ability to shape and customize the results of anything through small changes in their technique. Now I realize that is a bold statement. It's the reason I wrote this book. You'll find that the following chapters contain dozens of case studies proving time and time again that we are all capable of molding any situation in our favor. It doesn't require inborn talent or experience. The fact that we can dynamically move through life is our most powerful asset.

Whether your desire is to start a successful business, become a professional athlete, learn a new language, speed read at professional levels, quit your job, increase your income, pay off your home, maintain a huge savings account, or have enough freedom to travel the world, this book will give you every tool you need to do it.

Here are a few of the many points we'll discuss:

- How to accomplish just about anything you want in life by tweaking small items that make a big difference.

- Why most books will tell you to save, save, save in order to be wealthy while this book will teach you to save and spend your earnings, to be wealthy and happy.

- How I went from a 14 year old kid selling sunglasses to a multi millionaire just a few years later with no coaching, financial help or experience.

- Why life can be custom designed to whatever you want it to be. There is no pre existing template.

- An in-depth look at the results of dozens of case studies showing just how moldable the results can be in any area of your life, specifically:

  - Business. How to go from nothing to millions of dollars in revenue as a business owner in an industry you know nothing about. Over and over again.

  - Learning. How to learn to speed read and ace any test, within 30 days.

  - Sports. By tweaking just 3 things in each area and spending 25 days practicing, you'll learn to drive the golf ball 325 yards, serve a tennis ball 110 mph, ski the steepest mountain and sink three pointers from behind the line.

  - How to learn and accomplish anything your heart desires.

Have feedback or comments for me? Send an email to andrew@andrewrinehart.us and I'll do my best to respond (especially if you tell me you loved the book and you'll be sharing several copies with your loved ones)!

You can also visit www.andrewrinehart.us/blog to get more information on the Accomplish Anything techniques.

YOU ARE CAPABLE OF MORE THAN YOU KNOW

> "Life can be much broader once you discover that everything around you that you call life was made up by people no smarter than you. Once you learn that, you'll never be the same again"
>
> —Steve Jobs

I've worked with hundreds of thousands of people over the last ten years. They are from all walks of life. Some are rich, some are poor; some live in the United States and some live in other countries. Each one is different, yet they are all the same.

We all have the need to sleep, eat, and are subject to emotions and temptations. There is not one person on the planet that does not enjoy praise or the occasional indulgence. There are exactly the same amount of hours in a day, days in a week, and weeks in a month for all of us. Not one person has more or less time than another in any given year. We have brains and an erect body with free hands, allowing us to do things no other species on the planet can do. We have the same four basic needs: physical, intellectual, emotional, and spiritual.

We're all basically the same, yet the spectrum of success is so different.

How can this be?

How is it possible that two people, raised by the same parents, in the same house, with the same education, with similar IQ's, and similar physical appearances can achieve such drastically different results in life?

Isn't it frustrating to think of those now super-successful people, who were raised with less opportunity than you were? How did they do it?

PROTÉGÉS

Did God bless a few special individuals to be more successful than you? Are those people the way they are because of some kind of innate talent or ability? One thing is for sure, answering "yes" to those questions certainly makes us feel better. Answering "yes" satisfies the feeling of discomfort we get when we think that we might not have lived up to our potential. In fact, if you search "Why are human beings so <u>similar</u>?" on Google, the first several pages of results are articles about why human beings are so <u>different</u>. As a society, we don't want to even broach the subject as to why we're just as capable as anyone else. We'd rather assume that those that have achieved world-class success were destined to do so. The rest of us weren't born with the necessary talent so what's the point? Right? Or wrong...?

Geoff Colvin indicated in *Talent is Overrated* that Tiger Woods, even Mozart, may not have been examples of that "divine spark" we all love to pin point.

MOZART

Colvin points out that Mozart was raised by his father, Leopold Mozart, a famous composer and performer at the time. Leopold put his son through intensive music training starting at the age of three. Leopold also admitted that he "corrected" his son's work before anyone else saw it, he in fact dedicated so much time to his son that he (the father) personally stopped publishing music the same year his son began. Mozart's first four piano concertos, composed before he was eleven years old, contained no original music by him. They were put together out of the works of other composers.

By the time Mozart composed his first work regarded today as a masterpiece, he was twenty-one years old. At that point, he had been through eighteen years of extreme and expert training from a teacher that lived with him (and just maybe polished his work a little). Perhaps Mozart was more human than we all think. Perhaps it was something other than innate God given talent that put him on top.

TIGER WOODS

Earl Woods, Tiger Woods's father, wrote the book Training a Tiger. In it, Earl stated that he "loved to teach". Earl did not have any other children living at home when Tiger was born and was a self-confessed "golf addict". Earl and his wife decided that Tiger would "be the first priority in our relationship," at the time of his birth.

When Tiger was seven months old, Earl had already placed a putter in Tiger's hand. He put Tiger in a chair before the age of one and had him watch as Earl hit balls for hours on end. By age two, Tiger was on the course with custom clubs, playing regularly.

One of Tiger's childhood teachers later stated that when he first met Tiger, he felt "he was like Mozart."

EINSTEIN

He is regarded as the smartest man to have ever walked the earth. He was a "natural born genius" with an almost "mystery" like "gift". Yet Einstein didn't start out that way; at least not according to his family, early life peers and what history reports.

Einstein did not speak until 3 years old. His father was an engineer, although nearly every one of his business ventures failed leaving him to depend on relatives for support. When Einstein's father asked the headmaster what profession the boy should adopt, he said: "…it doesn't matter; he'll never make a success of anything".

Einstein failed his first admission examination to the Swiss scientific school he wanted to attend. Family friends said: "…that young man will never amount to anything because he can't remember anything".

Yet now, Einstein is hailed as the smartest man to ever walk the earth.

Is it possible that if Earl Woods had started Tiger out in baseball for instance, the same way he did with golf, that Tiger would have just as dominant in baseball? If the answer is yes, wouldn't that reverse the idea that Tiger is a natural-born, talented golfer? I believe the answer is indeed yes, but with a condition—Tiger adopted the Accomplish Anything techniques early on and probably didn't even know it.

For now, we can, at a minimum, agree that Mozart, Tiger and Einstein may have contributed to their own success more than the records have shown. This is great news. Performance, results, and success are more in our control than we may have thought.

But now what? Now that Tiger has had so much success and experience under his belt, what does he do now? Will he be great forever? Because he climbed the mountain more effectively than anyone else and has the experience, will he stay on top forever?

Guy Kawasaki, founder of Alltop.com, said in 2004 that: "…experience is vastly overrated…If you look at the greatest companies in the world, their founding members were unproven. In fact, they were clueless".

Are there people that have been playing golf longer than Tiger? Absolutely! But they aren't nearly as good. Are there people that have studied music composition as long as or longer than Mozart did? Sure, there's thousands. But they didn't accomplish nearly as much.

Are ongoing success, top performance, and world-class achievement related to something other than talent and experience? The harsh reality is actually not harsh at all: the results of anything we do are in our control. Talent, experience, money and education are not necessities. We can customize the results we get in just about any task in life. Stop thinking destiny and start thinking custom design.

The truth is, you can do everything Tiger Woods, Einstein, Mozart, Donald Trump, and even the Dali Lama has done. It's already in you.

Are there people with more experience, brains and money than you? Yes! But that doesn't mean a thing. You can blow right past them.

Most will say:

"You don't reach high levels of success without a high IQ."

"You need money to make money."

"Successful parents breed successful kids."

"Those with the best education will get the best jobs and be the most successful."

"You should only hire those with the most experience."

"Mozart was a genius from the second he was born".

Right? Wrong.

In short, we've specified a few things that don't make the necessary difference:

- Talent
- Inborn abilities
- Experience
- Money

But if all of these things don't matter as much as we thought, what things do?

WORKING BACKWARDS

Twenty years from now, you will be more disappointed by the things that you didn't do than by the ones you did do. So throw off the bowlines. Sail away from the safe harbor. Catch the trade winds in your sails. Explore. Dream. Discover.

—Mark Twain

Begin with the end in mind.

—Stephen Covey

I always liked beverages. I'm not sure why but energy drinks, soda, bottled water, you name it; I loved drinking it. Sometime around the age of 24, I decided that starting my own energy drink line would be a blast. I knew nothing about the industry nor did I have any connections. This was all the more reason to start one. I wanted to further prove my theory about custom made success, especially where no experience of talent existed. This project sounded perfect.

I contacted a manufacturing company that specialized in beverage inventions. I didn't want a template beverage, but one that was completely unique. I began laying out the color, texture, flavor, and what the benefits of consumption might be. At first, I wanted to develop a drink called *Pure* with a sky-blue color. Nothing like it existed. When I received my first batch of samples, the color instantly reminded me of *Windex* window cleaner, probably the last thing you want to be reminded of when drinking something. That was off the table and I went back to the drawing board. My second thought was a bright-red colored drink that had pomegranate flavoring. We'd go with the blue idea but implement that in to the can design not the color of the drink. My second batch of samples was perfect. The drink tasted like candy, delivered insane amounts of energy and because of the low sugar content, didn't cause an energy crash later.

I began uniquely marketing the drink and sold thousands of cans before it ever hit the market. I spent nothing in advertising up-front, but instead paid my consumers to refer the drink to their friends. All of the money spent came from ongoing revenue with very little up-front costs. Word got out and when the drink hit the market, I was selling 25,000 cans per week at nearly four dollars per can. Not bad. I was further convinced that a custom-designed life was possible. In honor of the idea, I called my line of drinks "Designer Beverages".

Because of the success of my first beverage, I became passionate about developing my second one. I needed more innovation and more creativity this time around. I studied the market, trends and future of the health and wellness industry, I looked for holes in supply where demand was high. I did hundreds and hundreds of hours of research and after all of it, came down to what I believed would be an absolute home run idea. The idea came initially from researching the success of Viagra and other sexual enhancement drugs on the market. For the first time, perhaps ever, sexual dysfunction was an openly discussed problem and one that needed fixing. Despite the open dialogue on the subject and success of Viagra, several countries around the world banned any medication or drug that contributed to the sexual dysfunction problem. Given my belief that most human beings are born with the same needs, hundreds of millions of people would likely be interested in getting a product that helped them in this area, just as millions had done in the US. I decided to develop and invent the world's first all natural sexual enhancement beverage for males and females. The key was that the beverage wouldn't be a drug; it didn't require a prescription, didn't come in pill form, didn't need approval from the FDA and was all natural. Anyone in the world could consume it with no side effects. It isn't the most conventional idea and it shocks most people at first but once you think about it, it makes a lot of sense. My research on the subject paid off. The idea was instantly a hit and just like the energy drink, thousands of people lined up before they had even tasted the drink. I visited the people in Singapore and Malaysia shortly after the launch of that product and hundreds came from all over Asia to thank me for finally producing such a beverage. I couldn't keep up with the orders, the demand was huge.

Hearing of our success, Playboy even went on to develop a spin-off of that beverage.

Later on, I developed an organic line of coffee and weight loss products. I wanted my company to be one that catered to dozens of different niches, weight loss, energy, health, and sexual dysfunction. Each of those categories carried the potential for billions of dollars in revenue. We went on to file a patent on the world's first all organic anti-aging coffee containing "adaptogens". I remember when I hit one-million cups of coffee sold. That was a great day.

The system worked but I still wasn't completely content. I believed that my next project would be the biggest I had ever engaged in and in order to make it great, I would have to focus 100% of my energy and focus on it. I sold the beverage company with all of the beverages mentioned to a publicly traded company in California in 2011.

My theories about the techniques of the Accomplish Anything techniques were cemented. It was time to tell the world.

HOW TO DO IT

Prior to launching the energy and sexual enhancement beverage line, I began jotting down my desired end-result (one million dollars in revenue, per month) and then worked backwards from there.

I compiled a list of questions so I could create my ultimate plan of attack. You should ask yourself similar questions whenever considering a new venture or an improvement upon an existing one. Always work backwards, that is, with the end in mind.

- At four dollars a can, how many cans would I have to sell to get to $1 million per month? Answer: 250,000

- If the average consumer were to consume one can per day (which was my goal), how many consumers would it take (drinking 30 cans per month) to get to 250,000 cans sold? Answer: approximately 8,300 consumers.

- In order to get 8,300 people sold on consuming my drink every day of every month, it would have to be a truly unique beverage experience. The main difference between my competitors and me was that I considered myself to be in the business of re-orders, not necessarily new orders. I wanted my customers to consume each and every day, day after day, month after month. How could I develop the world's greatest product in my niche area to help me accomplish this? Answer: I developed a unique referral based marketing method. People got paid to consume some amazing products as they referred more and more of their friends.

Once my product was developed and I had nailed down my end goal, it was all about marketing. How would I market the product with the highest return possible on my money invested? Was it wise to try and compete with Red Bull or should the marketing be done differently? Red Bull can clearly give away more free products than I can probably sell. Should I really be competing with them for shelf space in supermarkets or would a direct ship model work better? The direct sales model proved to be very effective and eliminated the need to try and compete with bigger names.

By clearly defining my desired end goals, I was able to focus in on that each and every day. Success quickly came and we far exceeded the original 8,300 desired consumers. My products became a hit in the United States, Dubai, Singapore, Malaysia, Australia, Canada, and several parts of Europe.

After you have a general idea about what the category in which you want to dominate, begin by defining your exact end goal. This may be becoming a professional athlete, putting $1 million in the bank, developing a business that produces $20,000 a month in profit or learning to speak a foreign language fluently. Write down your best case and just okay case. In other words, what would an enormous success look like and then whatever the next step down is, but would still be considered acceptable.

From there, develop steps that will get you to your end result like how many consumers does it take to get to $20,000 in profit per month in my industry? What does $1 million in profit mean in gross revenue and how do I get there?

Break your steps down in terms of monthly and then daily activity. What do I have to generate and accomplish each day and month to achieve my goal? How many days/months will it take me? Note: Your goal is not allowed to be "Save my money and work until I'm 65 at which point I'll retire and live the good life (AKA do nothing)".

Develop a team of people smarter than you. Lay out the goals clearly to your team and sell them on accomplishing certain items each day and month. It's critical that you teach them to think and work backwards with the exact same goals that you have.

Start a "pre-launch" campaign which involves the work ahead of the work. What can you do prior to beginning? This sets up your momentum and allows you to test the difficulty of a certain subject without risking too much.

Study the greatest. The power of the internet allows us to spy on anyone. Start studying the good (and the great) in your area of choosing and look for the differences between them. The differences will be small and most don't notice them. That's why most are good but few are great. Be deadly meticulous on this subject.

Work on one item at a time. Although the human being is capable of accomplishing anything, we are not capable of accomplishing them at the same time. If you try and do everything at once, you'll end up accomplishing nothing at all.

THE MOST EFFECTIVE SHORTCUTS TO SUCCESS

A QUESTION AND ANSWER WITH
MARK CUBAN AND MORE.

The human body and mind is capable of accomplishing things beyond a normal person's comprehension. It would stun you to learn what God had in mind when he created you. It would stun you even further to realize just how much more you could be doing.

Techniques, knowledge, methods and the correct practice are critical to getting you ahead in life. In fact, those four items will put you above 90% of the rest of the population. Most people simply are not willing to do more than the bare minimum. There are always short cuts, there are always loop holes and there is always a better way, you've just got to find it. Once you have all of those intact however, it's the effort that counts. You have to bury your head and work harder than the rest. Spending your entire life tweaking the tone of your voice in order to deliver what you believe to be better speeches will ultimately lead to your demise. Focusing on the wrong areas, ones that don't produce results will quickly lead to failure.

The surest shortcut to success is to work harder and exert more effort than everyone else. It will prove to be a shorter route than spending time trying to outsmart everyone, while they search for a shortcut.

There is no better example of this than a man from Texas. He was raised with very little, didn't get an Ivy League education, didn't inherit a dime and had to earn his successes through the acquisition of knowledge and sheer effort. Mark Cuban is, today, one of the few true billionaires on the planet.

In an exclusive interview for this book, I asked Mark about his thoughts on talent, the human ability to learn and what the true difference is between those that achieve world class results and the rest of us. Of course, the majority of the people believe that Mark probably came from rich parents and was born with a God given ability to run businesses, knowing when to sell and when to buy. In speaking with Mark, I learned that none of those are true. In fact, Mark spent the first 25 years of his life broke. He turned to heaving drinking in his mid 20's, slept on the floor of his friends apartment while dabbling in different business ideas and received absolutely no financial help from anyone. He got an incredibly later start in business than you or I probably did. Yet today, his net worth exceeds 2 billion dollars.

My first question for Mark was right to the point. I wanted to know what his thoughts were on talent. I asked, "Do you believe that you were born with a special talent to run businesses or become wealthy?"

"No," he replied. Extraordinarily short, but extremely meaningful.

Even Mark Cuban recognizes that he was not born with the ability to become wealthy. He learned it along the way. In his latest book, *How to Win at the Sport of Business*, Mark states that all of the information that he has gathered about business and wealth is the same information that anyone has; it's all completely public. He hasn't used any special tool or inside knowledge that isn't available to anyone, at any time, or in any place.

Mark explained his thoughts on learning like this: "In my humble opinion, once you have learned how to learn, then you can try as many different things as you want, recognizing that you don't have to find your 'destiny' at any given age."

"What's the true difference between people like you and the rest of the population?" I asked.

His answer once again came back simply: "Effort, preparation and focus."

Mark expands on the idea of effort by describing what he had to do to get his first business off the ground:

"I had to kick myself each day and recommit to getting up early, staying up late and consuming everything I possibly could to get an edge. I had to commit to making the effort to be as productive as I possibly could. It meant making sure that every hour of the day that I could contact a customer was selling time, and when customers were sleeping, I was doing things that prepared me to make more sales and to make my company better. Finally, I had to make sure I wasn't lying to myself about how hard I was working. It would have been easy to judge effort by how many hours a day passed while I was at work. That's the worst way to measure effort. Effort is measured by setting goals and getting results. What did I need to do to close this account? What did I need to do to win this segment of business? What did I need to do to understand this technology or that business better than anyone? What did I need to do to find an edge? Where does that edge come from, and how was I going to get there? The one requirement for success in our lives is effort. Either you make the commitment to get results or you don't."

Mark had only reinforced what I already knew; the very successful didn't always have an advantage over you. You can accomplish everything they have. And you can start right now. Desire, technique and the hunger for an edge seem to be major contributing factors in the amassing of Mark's fortune. You have those same desires burning inside of you right now and that's why you're reading this book. I asked my last question before ending the interview. "Which is more important, desire or talent?'

His answer shouldn't have surprised me, "Neither, effort trumps everything."

ADOPT THE BARBELL STRATEGY

You've probably heard it before. Most financial investors and "experts" will tell you something similar to this: "Invest in funds that have some aggressive methods and some that are more conservative. Overall, you'll get moderate and conservative positive results. You may hit it big with some of the more aggressive methods but if not, the conservative ones should be a sure bet."

Makes sense right? The truth is that this may sound great but few people are becoming wealthy in today's economy through these methods.

I spoke with a practicing doctor recently about his investments. Because he is mainly self-employed and his practice builds zero to little equity, he has been pile driving money into the stock market, short and long term bonds and mutual funds for years. He uses the biggest and most reputable firms in the nation to advise him. 15 years ago, he plotted down what he believed would be growth on top of growth. He calculated 10% interest on his money which was extremely conservative in his opinion given the current trends in the market. 10% per year for twenty-five years in addition to cutting out some of those "unnecessary" expenses like Starbucks coffee, a poor gas mileage vehicle and expensive vacations and he could retire comfortably at the age of 60. He would then be living the life that he always dreamed, relaxed, comfortable and set for life.

Needless to say, it didn't exactly go as planned.

The market took a downward turn in 2007. His stocks plummeted, his mutual funds tanked and his home was instantly worth half what he bought it for. He had not only cut out several of the things that made him happy (vacations, a nice car, coffee) but had lost 32% in his investments in the last twelve months alone. The last four years? His losses are over $1,500,000. He will not be retiring at sixty and will be lucky to get there by seventy, if at all.

Today, that doctor is left wondering if his money would have been worth more today had buried it in a cardboard box in his back yard instead of investing it. And it doesn't stop there. All these years, he could have enjoyed life just a little bit more. He could have driven that SUV that he really wanted and he could have taken more vacations with his family. Somewhere along the line, he got the impression that if he stopped spending $4.28 a day at Starbucks and instead invested that money in stocks, it would equate to millions of dollars someday. In reality, he lost money each time he put $4.28 in to the market in addition to losing out on the coffee. Personally, I'd rather have the coffee.

Times have changed. In fact, it may be time to fire your financial advisor all together and adopt the new barbell strategy.

WHAT IS IT?

The barbell strategy among the new class of the wealthy (the one I prefer) is a strategy that creates balance for your money, keeps it safe and gives you a much better shot at wealth, serious wealth. I'm not talking about 5%–10% returns annually in stocks that you can't control. I'm talking about 100%–1,000% returns on businesses that you do control.

The barbell method involves keeping your money in two places. The first is cash or cash equivalent. This, at an extreme level, can be money market accounts but only as long as they are liquid. Most people living by the barbell strategy keep their cash in bank accounts or something easily liquidated like gold and silver. Any of which are fine. Anything that can be liquidated for cash quickly and anything that you have at least some say or certainty in the value. Cash, although constantly depreciating through inflation, will probably not lose the majority of its value overnight. Stocks can.

The second place is putting money in to ventures on the opposite end of the barbell, or spectrum. These are what the public would consider "casino like risk" start up ventures. Ideally, you'll be the majority owner, you'll have a say over operations and you can influence the outcome and results with your efforts. The general public believes they're too risky because statistically, a start-up business has a high failure rate. There are no lack of articles online today suggesting that 90% of all small businesses fail in their first year. But is it considered a failure if you made money? What if you made enough money in the first year to close up shop?

Is that still considered a failure? I argue this subject all the time with people. One critical component of business ownership that the general public disregards is most entrepreneurs who keep at it eventually succeed. Their first business may fail, their second might as well. In fact, even if their first ten fail, and the eleventh succeeds, they'll live a better life than never having done it at all. The average person believes that small business ownership is too risky, which is exactly why they are average.

The barbell strategy doesn't involve putting your money in to any moderate or "in the middle" type of investment; its cash and its majority-owned businesses (mainly start ups). That's it. You have much greater control in either situation than you do investing in a publicly traded company you know very little about.

Suppose you have $20,000 to invest. You're contemplating an investment into a mutual fund that your neighbor told you about. "It should get 10% returns" he told you at the neighborhood barbeque. A 10% return on your money would be excellent in your opinion and you begin to get excited. After all, $2,000 profit per year (growing bigger each year exponentially) with no work would be great. You will have more than doubled your money in the next 10 years, assuming everything goes as planned. If you experience what the doctor experienced, you may lose it all but that seems highly unlikely as the fund "has performed excellently over the last 15 years".

Now suppose you took that same $20,000 and put it into a business of your own. This could be an affiliate based product website, a service oriented business with an hourly rate, a small retail store run by a profit sharing manager, a network marketing venture or any other business that can be started for $20,000 or less. Most can be operated with just 1-2 hours of work per day and some carry little to no overhead. Let's suppose that you achieve mediocre results in your small business, say $50 a day in profits, or $1,500 per month. At the end of one year, your total net earnings are $18,000. This doesn't seem like very much for a whole year, right? Not when compared to what your stock might have done in a great year. You just earned a nearly 100% return on your money in the first year. That doesn't exist in the stock market. Assuming you can continue with those profits for another year or two, your business will likely be worth 1-2 times gross yearly revenue, or $18,000–$36,000 to a buyer. Compared to a 10% return on an investment in which you carry no control, a small business venture dwarfs the potential returns on any other investment. What if your business fails and you lose the $20,000? It certainly could happen but remember, you'll always work the business backwards, as outlined in the chapter 2, and you'll only focus on businesses that you have some control over. The online world has opened up millions of possibilities allowing you to test the market before you enter in to it, lowering your risk by huge amounts. Regularly and before purchasing a rental property, I will run newspaper ads offering the home I'd like to buy as a rental, before I even own the property. I'll test the amount of calls I receive the quality of the potential renters and get a great feel for the market—all before spending a dime on the property. By the time I do purchase the property, I have renters lined up (usually creating a bidding war) and I know the home will rent immediately. I completely eliminate any question that I'll turn a profit on my property. This brings me to my next point, which is the last prong to the barbell strategy.

Many of you already have full time jobs and a family and are reading this thinking "I don't have the time for a start up business". If that is indeed the case, take that same $20,000 investment and use it as a down payment on a rental property. Feel out the market where the home is located by running "tester ads" and watch what can happen over 5-10 years while you build equity and the renters pay your mortgage for you. I've done this for years and continue to acquire more properties each quarter. The potential return on your investment far outweighs investing in an overseas penny stock or mutual fund run by someone you don't know.

After analyzing it all however, you may find that a few hours spent on a business of your own each evening is worth every second. The risk, the sacrifice, the potential riches, the game of it all, it drives me and keeps me going each day.

My most lucrative ventures have been start up businesses. In fact, I get asked several times a day which stocks I'm trading. The truth is I have never made one dime in the stock market, or bonds, mutual funds, or through the use of a financial advisor. Why would I invest in something that I have absolutely no control over? The world has transformed into a world of people who believe they can become rich by "brokering" deals. Everyone wants to make money on the transactions and business of everyone else. This is fine but the problem is somebody has to be the "creator" of these opportunities. Someone has to be buying and selling and not everyone can be brokering transactions. Online stock trading platforms, litigious law firms and business brokers alike, they all stand to make some money, but it will be at the expense of someone else.

Often times, they'll be the only ones that make money during a transaction completely unrelated to them.

If you take four things away from this chapter, let them be:

1. The surest way to become incredibly wealthy is through business ownership.

2. Creators make more money than connectors.

3. Begin adopting the barbell strategy into your life.

4. Effort trumps everything.

THE TRUTH ABOUT WHAT MAKES US GREAT

The amount of people attending shows in Las Vegas has gone down. The amount of people going to night clubs has gone up. This is evidence that people, in life, now want to be the show, not attend the show

—Steve Wynn

Practice does not make perfect. Only perfect practice makes perfect.

—Vince Lombardi

Like discussed earlier, Albert Einstein is regarded as the smartest man ever. He gave us many theories and insights into the world previously unknown. He wasn't always viewed with such high esteem however. Einstein struggled for years to find even decent employment and finally got work as a third-class government patent examiner. He was even said to have shown up to numerous business meetings with his pants on backwards.

Given that: his poor upbringing, other's doubts, and eccentric behavior, Einstein is a pseudo-god in the scientific community. Einstein went on to develop what we know today as the Theory of Relativity. He won a Nobel Prize in 1921 and is regarded today as the most influential genius of the twentieth century. Time Magazine named Einstein "Man of the Century" in 1999.

What does Albert Einstein have to do with you, your career, and your financial future? More than you may realize. Einstein's success is an excellent example of what I call, Results Based Training.

RESULTS BASED TRAINING (RBT)

At the age of twelve, I decided that I would become a professional golfer. Bold thought right? I played whenever I could, I spent hours on the range, played at numerous golf courses near my home and had all of the best equipment.

During my freshman and sophomore year in high school, I took the great Ben Hogan's advice and decided to put in more hours practicing than any of my peers. It was, as far as I could tell, the only way to get ahead. Hogan told stories of hitting balls late in to the night, at times until his hands bled. If I did the same, I was surely destined for greatness, right?

I woke up at 5:00 a.m. every day, six days a week to hit balls at an indoor driving range with nets (Utah weather did not allow for year round outdoor range practice). I spent nearly 40 hours a week practicing and this was in addition to my playing time. I did, as Hogan taught, literally hit balls until my hands bled. I spent more hours practicing than I did attending school. My goal was to become the best golfer in the state, get a college scholarship and then turn professional. With so much practice, how could I fail?

An odd thing transpired. My golf game actually got worse. My best competitive years were prior to the heavy practice and my worst years were during and after it. I stopped winning tournaments and then stopped placing in the top ten all together. I was absolutely devastated. Was all of that practice a waste? Actually, it was worse than a waste of time, it was actually damaging.

Without the ability to gauge my golf results (seeing where the ball went), I was engraining incorrect techniques and swing patterns. I was hitting into a net ten feet in front of me. I was getting progressively worse and worse at the game. The lack of real measurable results made my entire practice time void and damaged the progress I had made in the years prior. I was unable to see the ball's flight and wasn't even hitting off real grass. In my case, practice did not make perfect. The inability to gauge results made me much worse.

If you are not constantly able to gather results from your practice, you could be doing more harm than good. I'm not speaking on just sports either. Business, relationship, family, you name it. Gauge able data is critical to your success. It isn't merely the fact that you're doing something that makes you great but in how you are doing it that matters.

Tiger Woods, Albert Einstein, Jake Welch, Anthony Robbins, Steve Jobs, Michael Jordan, Tony Hawk, Jerry Rice, Donald Trump, Warren Buffett; they all have one thing in common and if you've been paying attention, it's not a God given innate ability to perform. It more has to do with the ability they have developed to focus intensely, work hard and gauge their results at extremely high levels as they go.

The importance of Results Based Training lies in literally every single success around the world. History will make you believe otherwise, particularly as events become more ancient. It's romantic to believe that Jake Welch was the smartest kid growing up and was born with the ability to manage. It's magical to think that Warren Buffet has a God given talent to allocate capital. It's inspiring to believe that Mozart was a musical genius at birth. But none of that would be true. All of those individuals incorporated RBT and in many cases, did so obsessively.

VIDEO DUPLICATION

Whether its public speaking, business or sports, using the power of video recording to gauge your results is one of the quickest ways to improve at anything. During the case study phase of writing this book, I taught myself how to do a dozen things that I was previously completely unfamiliar with. How? I watched the experts on YouTube, tried to copy what they did, filmed myself doing it and then compared my video and their video. Sound simple? It is. You'll be astonished at how quickly you can become good by closely mimicking the actions of the great.

Human beings are capable of developing any skill and that capability is enhanced with the power of visualization and emulation.

The steps:

- Watch world class performers on video. Use Youtube.com and Vimeo.com. When it comes to sports, pick out the athletes that have a body type similar to yours.

- Spend 15 minutes filming yourself doing exactly what they do (or as close as you can possibly get). For recording, I prefer the Flip HD camera but even the video camera on your cell phone will do.

- Compare your video to theirs, side by side, and take note of the differences.

- Repeat.

SERVE LIKE A PRO

It was a warm fall afternoon in Utah and a friend suggested that we try playing tennis. I instantly thought of how boring tennis appeared on TV. I would change the channel instantly if the horrific sport ever accidentally showed up on my screen. Somehow however, I was convinced that day to try it out.

That day was the first time I had ever picked up a tennis racket. I didn't know how to hold it, what the rules were and frankly, could barely get the ball over the net accurately. I couldn't hit the ball consistently in the center of the racket which inevitably sent balls flying off in every direction. How embarrassing.

I left that day further convinced that I had been right about tennis all along. Then it hit me, what a perfect opportunity to apply the video duplication techniques this would be. I was so horrible at the game that putting the techniques to the test would prove to be the ultimate verifier.

Firstly, I sat down to decide what I wanted my end goal to be. I had heard that pros serve the ball at 100 MPH or greater. That seemed like a good goal for me. I ordered a radar speed gun from Amazon.com to gauge my results. Time frame allotted for my goal: 60 days.

That night, I found the best rated tennis player with a body size closest to mine, Roger Federer. I studied his serve playing it back from every angle over and over again (there is no lack of these on Youtube. com), then I played it in slow motion. I put it up on my TV screen and with a racket in hand, tried to follow and match the various positions of the racket throughout the serve, pausing the video throughout to check myself. Because I had no experience or coaching in the game, I could easily change how I would have naturally believed serving should have worked. I had not previously engrained any bad habits, I was completely moldable.

Next, I hit the tennis court again; this time with the video camera on my iPhone recording my every move. I served over and over again trying to emulate exactly what Federer did. I filmed myself from behind, the side and in front. At first it was difficult but I could quickly see that his elbow and hips were in quite unique positions at impact, not like normal club players. The more I tried to get as close to that as possible, the more my serve started to improve. First, it got faster, and then it grew more accurate. 1 hour in to my first session and I was already considerably better. I had hoped they would initially be better but my serves were clocking at about 45 MPH, far short of my goal. I had a long way to go.

I went home and put my serve up on the computer screen next to his. I played both in slow motion right next to each other. I was still way off course but certainly better than I had been the first day. I decided to focus on Federer's hips and elbow positions. They (and other pros) were in the same position each time he made impact, much different from where mine were. I spent 20 minutes that night doing dry swings in my living room with the racket only.

The next day, I took to the court again. This time, I had Federer's swing burned into my memory. Just in case I forgot, I had my laptop with me for a refresher view.

My swing began to improve, rapidly. By aligning my hips with the service line on the court (also the net) at the time of impact, I ensured that I got a full hip rotation. My upper body responded almost like a coil and my speeds picked up instantly. Secondly, by dropping my right elbow down and away from my body as much as possible, I was able to take full advantage of long arms, like a whip snapping at the tip. These 2 items alone increased my serve speed by 55 MPH. I was now consistently serving at 90 MPH just 4 days in to my testing.

By emulating Federer's swing and repeating the video duplication process, I began serving the ball over 100 MPH consistently and accurately just 41 days after picking up a racket for the first time, I had accomplished my end goal 19 days ahead of schedule. My fastest serve recorded was 111 MPH. I joined a tennis club and began competing. What's so exciting about this technique is that not only did it teach me to become an excellent tennis player but also taught me to love the game. I will surely be playing for the rest of my life and I continue to use the video duplication method to improve everyday.

APPLY IT TO BUSINESS

The same process can be applied to business. In place of video, find a mentor, especially in areas where you have no expertise. Study his/her every move, emulate and then gauge your results consistently. Remember, more time spent doing something doesn't necessarily equate to improvement. Practice does not make perfect, perfect practice (results based training) does.

Whether it's in becoming an expert tennis player, driving the golf ball 300 yards, learning a foreign language, speaking in front of audiences of 1,000 plus or learning to ace that reading test, it can all be done using the technique of video duplication. Even silly things like learning to juggle can be accomplished within 22 minutes.

Can you imagine where my golf game would be today had I used these techniques back in my High School days, instead of beating balls mindlessly against a net?

Where would your career be if you constantly emulated the industries best, everyday?

Are you just going through the motions of the day, trying to please your boss and get to the weekend?

What would happen if you decided that you will become the absolute best at what you do, and start now?

How would your life change?

MEET CHAD NETHERLAND

Have you ever met a man that can rip a phone book in half with his bare hands? How about someone that can hold back a plane from taking off with only his arms and a chain? Neither had I.

Chad Netherland was born in the early 70's in Biloxi Mississippi. Seemingly, he was just like any other child, interested in new things, playful and full of energy. His father was the owner of a martial arts studio and Chad began to take an interest in fighting, lifting and strength. There was only one problem, Chad was born with a heart murmur and none of the above activities came easy. Worse, Chad severed numerous tendons in his left hand when he was 10 years old. The doctor told him he'd have to undergo surgery and would never have any grip strength in his left hand.

How would Chad live on to be great in the family business without any grip strength? You'll ask yourself that question when no sooner, Chad will remove a deck of cards from his pocket and rip them in half vertically with his bare hands. He is one of only four people in the world that can do that. In fact, Chad went on to do several things that involved grip strength, and a lot of it. He became number one in the world in each category, literally.

Chad's current list of World Records broken is:

1. Longest duration to hold back two aircrafts from taking off by hand

2. Fastest time to break 50 blocks of ice

3. Most ice broken in a single strike. 20 blocks equating to 16 feet of ice

4. Bed of nails concrete block break. 848.10 pounds of concrete broken with a 16 pound sledgehammer (record broken 6 times)

5. Fastest handcuff escape

6. Fastest time to bend 10 nails by hand (21.13 seconds)

7. Fastest time to tear 10 decks of cards by hand (46 seconds)

So how did Chad accomplish all of this when the odds seemed to be against him? In interviewing him for this book, he stated several things that got my attention. In fact, he emphasized the need for results based training before I even showed him the final copy of this book. He talked about the need to set goals as you go and constantly be gauging results and evolving. When I showed him the exact techniques of RBT, he said "that's exactly what I've been doing and my competitors have not".

I asked Chad how important technique was in his accomplishments: "Can you teach anyone to do what you do?" I asked.

His response: "Proper technique is everything. Being able to execute that technique flawlessly without hesitation is where the true mastery comes into play. I hold the world record for breaking the largest stack of ice in the world with a single strike, 20 blocks that were over 16 feet deep and weighed over 2,000 pounds. With the proper training and dedication, I can teach anyone to break that ice."

He took a break from the interview and bent a frying pan into what looked like a rolled up burrito. "Want me to drive a nail through a board using my hand?" he asked? "That's okay", I said, I got the point.

Needless to say, Chad truly has proven that human beings are capable of accomplishing anything, even against all odds. And it doesn't stop there. If you ask Chad what his favorite broken world record is, he says "the next one". On the subject of practice, Chad states "practice makes permanent, perfect practice makes perfect".

Chad is currently training to push an H2 Hummer for a mile in the fastest ever recorded time.

What would that doctor that told him he'd have no grip strength be saying now?

DOES PRACTICE REALLY MAKE PERFECT?

Repetition may work when memorizing lines for a play or words in a song. However, studies have shown that doing the same thing over and over can actually hinder you rather than help you.

Think about it on this level. Recently, we have seen an influx in extreme fitness regimens. They tout that, by following their DVD workouts and diet plan, in thirty, sixty, and ninety days you too can be at your fitness peak! Their biggest buzzwords? Muscle confusion.

As it turns out, muscle confusion is a scientifically proven methodology to improve your muscle tone and keep your body guessing. It will always be "on its toes," so to speak; constantly working and burning calories.

Going out to the batting cages and swinging for hours on end is not the way to become a super star baseball player. It takes more than your ability to swing a bat to be a good player. Do you understand the rules of the game? Do you know the amount of force it will take to stop a baseball coming toward you at various velocities? Do you know the right angle to hit the ball so it will not be counted as "foul"?

In order to achieve greatness in whatever it is you want—whether it is in a sport, business, or education—you must work at from every angle imaginable. Continuously change your perception.

IN A NUT SHELL

"When desire dies, fear is born"

—Balthazar Grecian

"Nothing stops the man who desires to achieve.
Every obstacle is simply a course to develop
his achievement muscle. It's a strengthening
of his powers of accomplishment."

—Eric Butterworth

In 2007, the University of Michigan con-
ducted a study that should have changed the way we
view desire entirely, although it did not. The study
discovered that although fear and desire are viewed as
psychological opposites, they actually share the same
brain kernel. A tiny portion of the brain can retune its
functions from moment to moment, bouncing back
and forth between fear and desire, depending upon
our environment. For example, bright lights and loud,
unfamiliar, music might cause us to feel fear. A comfortable, quiet, and familiar environment might cause
us to feel desire. The exact same circuit in the brain
can literally switch back and forth in micro-seconds.
More important than any of that, they discovered

that we have control over which one we feel. This is extremely empowering.

Fear paralyzes. It's like poison. There's no use for it. Desire, however, is like adrenaline. Skillfully applied desire can put you in a position to Accomplish Anything you like. Very simply: desire sets the winners apart from the losers. Desire is the absolute most important characteristic you can develop and take away from this book. It will prove to be the springboard into the rest of the principles found here. It is the first and most important stepping stone. Without it, the rest of this book (or any other book) is completely useless. With it, the techniques found in the next chapters will be your main focus.

Let's look at a few scenarios that happen every hour of every day, around the world.

A man gets laid-off from his job. His family struggles to keep food on the table and his home is on the verge of foreclosure. Suddenly, and at the last moment, he finds his dream job and turns things around.

A single mother of three with no experience in the business world and under heavy financial stress thinks of a new product for the fashion industry. It becomes a blockbuster product and she retires from that one idea.

The economy is faltering and a business owner is struggling to keep his company afloat. They are in their final days before filing bankruptcy and the owner lands a huge contract to save the company.

We've all heard stories like this. What if we could tap in to this kind of "magic" everyday, not just in times of crisis? Just how different would our lives be?

I call these times of super human achievement (attained during times of crisis) the "flow". The truth is we can manipulate our own body and mind into believing that we're fighting for our lives each and every day. The reality is that we are doing exactly that. The results you'll gain during times of the flow are far greater than what you'd normally receive. Once you've convinced yourself that success is the only option, you'll be shocked at what your true spirit is capable of achieving.

THE FLOW

1. You've decided upon an achievement, goal or possession that you must have. Let's go with something straight forward, a new car, say a Maserati. Price tag–$100,000.

2. You have absolutely no idea how you'll come up with $100,000. After all, you're getting by okay, not falling behind but not getting ahead, but you certainly don't have an extra $100k lying

around to spend on a sports car. Regardless of that fact, you'd love to own a Maserati.

3. Substitute the desired item (the Maserati) with something that would leave you no choice but to obtain. Perhaps you have kidney failure and the only matching donor is to charge you $100,000 for a new kidney. You either come up with the money or you put your life at risk. This is a critical part in the process. If you aren't tackling projects in "crisis" mode, you'll be lazy and apathetic about the results.

4. You open a new bank account for your venture. This account is to be solely for the purpose of achieving your desired goal. No money is to enter or leave the account unless it is related to this project.

5. A deadline is to be set for the attainment of your new "kidney". You should have 4 milestone goals along the way, so you stay on track.

6. Make your goal known to the public, along with the deadlines. Tell your family and friends, and do it in a setting where a large group is gathered. Make it an announcement. Let them know how serious you are and that failure is not an option (you don't have to reveal

the actual end goal yet, just that you are trying to come up with x amount of dollars before xyz date). Family party coming up? Perfect opportunity. You need a public resolution to convince your inner being that failure is not an option.

7. You must create an income on top of and in addition to what you're making now, in order to begin depositing money in to your new bank account. You'll begin to look at creative ways to finance a new piece of rental property, a home based business that you can run in your spare time (network marketing, affiliate marketing, blogging, an eBay business), an inexpensive product invention or any job that can be done in your spare time that will produce a commission (you can get any job in the world as long as you deliver the value first, see the story of my first cell phone job in the introduction of this book for a perfect example).

8. Because failure is not an option and because you're passionately working in crisis mode, your brain, body and soul will respond with adrenaline and focus not normally delivered in your everyday tasks.

9. You'll begin to look outside the box. You'll begin to develop relationships with people you never knew before. Because you made your goal public, you'll begin to receive guidance, tips and support from people inspired by your announcement. The more people you talk to about your goal, the more doors will open up.

10. Lastly, you'll passionately and without hesitation or embarrassment seek advice and council from those that already have acquired your goal. You'll emulate their successes and ignore their weaknesses.

Remember, the flow works for anything you want. Your brain doesn't know the difference. Instead of a Maserati, plug in a happy marriage, great kids, a vacation, a new home, a better job, early retirement, a 300 yard golf drive or a perfect score on a foreign language test. The power to achieve is already in you. The only thing left is tapping in to that ability.

For more tips on the power of the flow, send me an email at andrew@andrewrinehart.us or look at my blog at www.andrewrinehart.us/blog. I see thousands of people each month accomplish their dreams through this method. But it truly only works if you "burn the boats" and make success the only option.

HOW TO GET WHATEVER YOU WANT

"You will get all you want in life if you help other people get what they want"

Most of the time, what we want will orig-inate from someone or something else. We want more love and affection, more money, more appreciation from our boss or co-workers, a bigger home, more free time, the list goes on. In most cases, these things will come from another person. So how do you get what you want, if you're not the one in control of accessing it? If you want to influence the actions of another person, you have to be the first to act.

Life is a "reap what you sow" business. You get out of it what you put into it. Want more love? Give it. Want more friendship? Give it. Desire more money? Put yours to work. You must take action and must be the one that moves first. The key word here is reciprocity, except you cannot wait for the other person to act first. You create the reciprocity. I can guarantee you increased success when putting this in to practice. If you're waiting for things you want to fall in your lap, get comfortable because you won't be going anywhere soon.

Let's suppose you want to go in to business with Joe. If you approached him and said "Joe, I'd love to partner with you and have you represent my products. I think I can make a lot more money," you're doomed. Find a way to increase his business and make him more money first, and you'll be shocked at what will take place on the back end. You'll get what you want. Those seeking instant gratification will struggle with this first step.

Now, approach Joe from a different angle. "Joe, I want to partner with you. But, I know what a huge risk this would be on your part. I'd like to work for you, help your business grow, and prove myself to you before trying out a joint venture."

By helping others in their business, you're increasing your chances of getting what you want later. Think about the people in life you want to be like. Maybe it's a CEO or the owner of a company who's now retired, living on a beach somewhere. Now, what did that person do in order to get to where they are? Did they sit back and let someone else take the reins? Did they let fear keep them from taking risks? Did they go to others looking only to advance themselves? No! They went out and did something. They were proactive. They worked with others to get their ideas moving.

It doesn't matter that you're doing something; it matters how you are doing it.

REVERSE THE RISKS

The main reason people don't take action is because they're scared of the consequences. To get what you want, you need to be able to remove the caution from another person. In marketing, this would be the offering of a money back guarantee on your products. The guarantee permits the customer to send back the product and takes the risk off of them and puts it on you. When trying to get what you want, do everything you can to remove the risk of the opposite party. Everybody has walls of caution and in this day and age, they're sky high.

You've got to learn how to break down those walls. Offer them a way to pay you nothing unless you perform. Use that as the driving force behind your work. Work like your pants are on fire and the only way to extinguish them is to keep your "personal stock" growing!

You've got to work for it! Remember my story about working for the cell phone store? I had no idea how to sell anything and no experience whatsoever. The owner of the store could have scoffed and turned me away when I told him what I wanted. Honestly, I wouldn't have blamed him. I was a fifteen year old kid with no retail experience. I told him I wanted to market his products and would do so being paid whatever he wanted. He was accustomed to hundreds of people applying for jobs with demands such as health benefits, a 401k package, and a high salary, so he gave me a chance because he had nothing to lose. I completely reversed every potential risk he could have had. I delivered value first and got paid second. You can have any job (and just about anything) in life using this same technique.

I went on to become the number one sales rep in the company, then in the country, then opened my own store and finally, opened more than one hundred fifty stores, all before I turned twenty-five year old.

Can you imagine what would have happened had I only sought what I wanted at the time (instant money)? He would have told me to get in line with the hundreds of others applying. I would have been lost in the shuffle with countless applicants, many with decades of experience.

I owe, in part, the success of that business to the ability I had at the time to remove the risk on his part. He had nothing to lose by giving me a chance, but everything to gain.

Mitigate other's risk whenever you can and watch the items that you desire flow towards you. By lessening the risk on others, you gain trust and credibility. Continue to enrich that credibility and nothing will be beyond your grasp.

Remember to keep your emotions in check. Hatred, jealousy and fear are paralyzing. More importantly, they are extremely self-defeating. These things can blind you and will never allow you to get what you truly want. Emotions are tricky. Do not get drunk off of them. Emotions can make you think you're an idiot when you're not, and a genius, when you're really a dunce. Keep the logical part of your mind aware and open at all times. Remember to operate with logic instead of emotions. Emotions can keep you from attaining your goals. Keep this in mind when others are ruled by their emotions during business deals.

WINNING

> "Winning is not a sometime thing; it's an all
> the time thing. You don't win once in a while,
> you don't do things right once in a while, you
> do them right all the time. Winning is a habit.
> Unfortunately, so is losing."
>
> —Vince Lombardi

Does it really matter if you are number
one? Does it really matter if you shoot to the top? I
mean isn't number two or even number fifty still good?
Won't you still flourish in your industry or sport, make
a great living and be perfectly happy if you're number
one hundred? Are the benefits to being number one
over being number fifty all that different?

As it turns out, yes. It's enormously different.

In the book "The Dip", Seth Godin explains why
being number one is seriously underrated.

"Our culture celebrates superstars. We reward
the product or the song or the organization or the
employee that is number one. The rewards are heavily
skewed, so much so that it's typical for number one to
get ten times the benefit of number two, and a hundred times the benefit of number three."

Taking a graph from Seth's book, we easily see the difference between being number one and being number two in the ice cream industry.

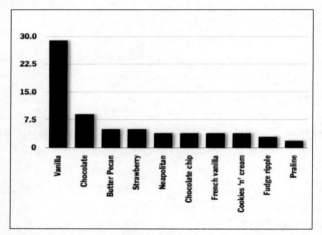

As you can see, it pays to be the number one ice cream, and it doesn't just pay you a little more than the competition, it pays you a lot more. People love a love story, we love a winner and more importantly, we're willing to reward those winners big time.

It isn't just ice cream or movies or actors that fall in to the "it's worth it to be number one," category. Just about everything does. It applies to resumes, college applications, best selling records, athletes, business owners, employees, mothers, fathers, husbands, wives and everything in between. The number one spot always flourishes because the market place rewards them continuously.

Seth goes on to say:

"People don't have a lot of time and don't want to take a lot of risks. If you've been diagnosed with cancer of the navel, you're not going to mess around by going to a lot of doctors. You're going to head straight for the "top guy", the person who's ranked the best in the world. Why screw around if you get only one chance. When you visit a new town, are you the sort of person who wants to visit a typical restaurant, or do you inquire the concierge for the best place? When you're hiring someone for your team, do you ask your admin to give you the average resume, or do you ask him to screen out all but the very best?"

As a result of our intentionally narrowing the results, the number one position is rewarded far more than the #2 spot is. Everyone naturally does the narrowing, not just you.

ARE YOU NUMBER ONE?

Number one can mean a lot of different things for a lot of different people. It isn't always as cut and dry and as who sells the most ice cream. The real and more important fact is this; most people never get to number one because they settle. They settle for less than they can truly achieve. They settle for less than what they can truly have. They settle for a mediocre spouse because "nobody better showed up". They settle for a mediocre family because "kids will be kids". They settle for a mediocre income because "God gave more talent to that other guy and that's just the way it". They settle for a mediocrity in just about everything and this is why they are not number one in anything.

Want to become a millionaire as a financial planner? What's the difference between what you do and what the number one performers do every 10 minutes throughout the day?

Want to get promoted at your current job? Name 5 specific things that the last person that got promoted did and do the same things, but better and with your own individuality. Take to the internet to spy on the number one performers.

Want to retire early and travel the world? How much money would that take? What can you do to put that amount of money in the bank and in how much time? Whatever those numbers are, they're likely outside of your comfort zone and experience level. You're going to have to push yourself.

Want to become a world class athlete? Find the number one athlete in your sport, with a similar body type to yours, and study his/her every move. Use the techniques of RBT and video duplication. Set time frames and go to work with razor sharp focus.

Are you a number one husband or wife? What can you do to improve and make sure that your significant other has a number one spouse?

The truth is you have the power to be number one. Your passion, whatever it may be, has someone claiming right to the number one position. You can probably think of his/her name immediately. Maybe it is an individual or maybe it's a corporation but either way, it exists. They're likely doing better than you are right now but believe me; they are no smarter than you are. You have available to you all the same resources that they did at one point. The only difference between you and them is that they discovered the techniques required to mold the results of projects as they progressed. They understand that the results we get in life can be custom designed to whatever we want.

BUSINESS IS CHANGING, START ADAPTING

The way we do business is changing right in front of our eyes. The new generation of wealth creators is faster and sleeker than ever before. If you're not paying attention and evolving right along with them, you'll get passed up for promotions, job offers, and even raises.

If you read The Millionaire Next Door, you'll begin to believe that giving up your Starbucks coffee each day in order to save four dollars will put millions of dollars in your bank account forty-two years from now. The sad truth is: those days are over. The very basis of that theory was one thing; compounded growth on your money through the power of interest. What if there is no interest? What if saving/investing your money actually costs you through losses or inflation? I can't tell you how many people I know personally that have lost twenty years of savings in just the last three years. That money would be worth more today had it been buried in a box in your backyard.

The days of beefing up a 401(k), investing your savings in low-yield bonds, and assuming your home is your biggest asset may, unfortunately, be over. The even worse news? It may never go back to the way it was when Thomas Stanley wrote that book. However, with my help, you can make more money now than ever before.

Get plugged in! Communication is faster and more effectively than ever before. Skype, Facebook, and Twitter allow us to communicate with hundreds of thousands of people from all over the world, every single day.

The older generation communicates with, maybe, twenty people per day. The new generation understands that it may be better to develop cyber-relationships with thousands, compared to personal relationships with a few. This means more casual, less stuffy way of conducting business. This does not sit well with the older, suit-wearing, business minds. Thousands of companies are now doing hundreds of millions of dollars in sales before they ever even meet a customer personally. Communication is changing in a big way, whether we like this or not.

The new business minds understand that nearly every industry and product can be offered online for cheaper. Proof of this is everywhere. Blockbuster

Video entered into bankruptcy, in part because of online competitor Netflix. Borders Bookstores closed down entirely because of Amazon.com; Barnes and Noble is next. Publishers have begun to feel the pressure from a recently announced publishing addition to Amazon.com. E-books are starting to outsell hardcopy books. The amount of garage sales across the country decreased because of the rise of eBay. Brick and mortar cell phone stores began to disappear because of "candy machine-like" vending machines that offer phones cheaper. The vending machines are then phased out because wireless providers improve their online ordering and drop shipping programs. As a result, Sprint absorbed Nextel, T-Mobile absorbed Voicestream and AT&T absorbed Cingular. The entire industry consists of just three service providers.

Investing $5,000 into the stock market will produce no where near the returns that $5,000 will in a business of their own. And giving up their morning Starbucks run to save a couple of bucks? Ridiculous. That's the one hour they can network with important clients and customers, catch up on emails, and plan out their day. They communicate their message and promote their product to thousands of people through social media postings and email responses during that one hour alone! Besides that, the up and coming business minds do not believe that retirement should be ten, twenty, or thirty years from now. They are going to enjoy life (and their coffee) as they go.

The richest people in the world are business owners. Yes, the world needs good employees, but, you must also understand that you can be both. By looking for start-up and ownership opportunities, it allows you to have a say in operations. They are incredibly smart, insightful and resilient. The "plugged in" generation of business owners should only take advice from only those people that have produced better results than them.

You've got to understand that, no matter what your age, the world is going to continue to change and you need to be willing to change right along with it. "Tug boat" businesses can be more powerful than "cruise ships" because they can maneuver quicker. Information is power and technology is vital.

The harsh reality is actually not harsh at all. We can embrace the new methods of wealth creation easier than ever before. We can automate and duplicate anything with the power of technology. The profit potential is endless. There are no "hours of operation" anymore. We're using every second of every day more effectively and our future is brighter than it's ever been.

The next time you need to leave work early to run an errand, go shopping, or beat traffic, stop and think about what you're really doing. You are, essentially, putting your work and wealth creation on hold. Just imagine how much money you could be making by paying someone else to do the task while you continue to produce income.

Even if your hourly income is twenty dollars, you should never again mow the lawn, go to the dry cleaners or change the oil in your car. There are plenty of folks willing to do these for less than what you would be making by not doing them. So the next time you are faced with a task, any task, ask yourself – What's it really costing me? Keep this in mind when you are tempted to look for coupons in the Sunday newspaper and then run all over town to save three dollars on laundry detergent. Tasks like this will suck your life, and income producing hours, away. Believe it or not, this one technique can make a huge difference in deciding whether or not you become on of the super successful.

You don't necessarily need to "save" your way to wealth. To become wealthy, you must have the ability to change or influence other people. This is just a fact. I don't know anyone that is wealthy that hasn't created massive change in the lives of others. Money comes from one place: other people.

SO HOW IS IT DONE?

How can you influence others and bring out their inner greatness, as well as yours? The answer may not be as difficult as you think. To create a massive change in someone's life, only a few of your behaviors need to change. It does not have to be difficult. The key here is this: a lot of change can come from altering just a few behaviors. You simply have to focus on the right things. Let's look at an example that shows us what not to do. I find this is sometimes the best way to learn.

EXAMPLE:

The United States has a huge drug problem. Each day, millions of dollars worth of illegal drugs are produced and sold in our country. A large portion of these are brought in from foreign lands. Drug use is directly related to crime, which is directly related to the well-being of our citizens, which in turn, is directly related to our economy. The ripple effect puts our health and our economy at huge risk.

The current method in place to deal with the drug problem is heavy punishment for producing, selling or using illegal drugs. We are almost 100% focused on cutting off the supply. We put producers of drugs in jail, we burn their fields and we seize their buildings. We figure that if we cut off the supply, the demand will magically disappear. This is just not the case. As long as there is a demand, someone is going to figure out how to supply it. No matter what the cost.

(On a side note, why would anyone use marijuana? The world will reward you for being fast and smart, not slow and stupid).

By focusing on the actual vital behaviors driving this problem, I believe we could make leaps and bounds towards solving the issues.

Instead of using the above method of "cutting off the supply," what if we instead focused on cutting off the demand? What if we focused our money on educating people about how drugs will ruin their life? What if we triple our anti drug education efforts in public schools? If there was no demand, we would never have to worry about cutting off the supply again. By focusing on the behavior behind the supply and not the behavior behind the demand, we're getting nowhere. In fact, it's just getting worse. We could be spending the next one hundred years chasing down drug dealers when we could be going about it a different way.

With regard to the smaller, more immediate picture: what are you doing in life that is helping to alter the vital behaviors of those you wish to do business with? It is critical that you answer this for yourself.

ARE YOU TRYING TO INCREASE RESULTS BY INCREASING PUNISHMENT?

One of the most consistent behaviors behind the wealthy is their ability to instill positive reinforcement. The wealthy teach and lead with positivity. The poor say things like "Didn't I just tell you that five minutes ago?" or "I can't believe you messed up again!"

If you truly want to increase your net worth, start positively changing the vital behaviors of those around you. Your results will triple, guaranteed.

THE DISCOMFORT ZONE

My entire life has been dedicated to stud-ying and running businesses. I did it at an early age so that I could become free later on in life. The rewards were even better than I thought. Throughout that journey, I have studied the key but small differences between the average and the super successful. We've talked about a lot of the things that make a key difference in finding that success in this book. One thing however stands out perhaps above all of them. That is the ability that the super successful have in dealing with pain and discomfort.

It doesn't matter what you stand up for, it's the very fact that you are standing up for something that will get you enemies, will cause you pain, will give you anxiety and create problems you didn't expect. Most of your plans will be derailed, if not all of them.

If you can prepare yourself to be able to handle discomfort, you'll instantly jump ahead of 99% of the population that simply is not willing to deal with it. No one wants to leave their comfort zone and this is why they fail, because they never tried at all. Our biggest failures lie in the things we were too scared to try. In most cases, it's because we were too comfortable in our current, and in most cases, average, ventures.

Each day, I try to work inside of what I call "The Discomfort Zone" at least 3 times. It might only constitute 1 total hour throughout the day but I can ensure you that it is during this tiny sliver of time that true wealth is created.

The Discomfort Zone begins at times when you least expect it, that's what makes it uncomfortable. It might be 5:30 p.m.and you're still in the office. Everyone has gone home for the day and you push on for another hour making 10 more calls, resulting in higher commissions for the month. It might be during a popular football game the nation is watching but you decide to spend time improving your online brand image. It will probably occur when people start attacking you personally or legally. Your blood will boil and you'll wonder if this is the life you really want. It is during those times that most give up and few push through.

The level of pain and discomfort we can deal with is one of the most important determiners of how successful we'll ultimately be.

In fact, I find that when I constantly and purposefully try and push myself into activities of discomfort, those activities become ones of pleasure within a short period of time. I look back on my previous fear and wonder what the big deal was. This is the truest example of the body's ability to dynamically move through the many events that life can throw us. We truly are living a dynamic life.

4 THINGS EVERY ENTREPRENEUR SHOULD FOCUS ON

As you prepare to become an insanely successful entrepreneur (entrepreneurs hold the majority of the wealth in the world so this is the goal), you will be analyzing opportunities on a consistent basis. Having the ability to decipher which are good and which are not is critical to your success. You'll end up passing on 90% of them and that's not a bad thing.

I ask myself 4 questions each time a new venture is presented to me. I encourage you to think "CDMA" when ever an opportunity comes your way.

C is for Control. You need to have some amount (the majority is preferred) of control over revenue, expenses and bottom line profits. If you don't have a say in where the money is going, avoid it. If you can't improve the revenue with your own actions, keep looking. This includes avoiding complicated silent partnerships and penny stocks.

D is for Duplication. You will not achieve true wealth selling cars yourself, underwriting mortgages yourself, selling real estate yourself, practicing law yourself, running a retail store yourself…or a million other things that will completely consume you. You absolutely must have the ability to duplicate yourself and your efforts. There are simply not enough hours in the day. You need an army to make serious money in today's world. There are increasingly fewer "independently wealthy" individuals in the country today.

M is for Margins. This is one result of having the correct amount of control. I've run businesses that do 10 times less gross revenue than my competitors, yet my bottom line profits are far greater than theirs. You must be a master of margins. Stop thinking about increasing revenue (when typically, only 10%-20% of that will actually equate to profits) and start thinking about increasing the bottom line. When you do, the gross will take care of itself. This is accomplished by focusing on the center and biggest piece of your income statement.

A is for Automation. This ties in to duplication. If you can duplicate and automate a profitable system or product (even if it's pennies in profit), you'll be wealthy beyond your dreams. Your efforts will only go so far. The efforts of other people will never end.

I put each business I look at through the "CDMA Test". If it meets each of the 4 above requirements, I've got something interesting that probably deserves more due diligence.

I've run several CDMA approved businesses. My first was through franchising, an incredibly powerful business platform. It duplicated around the country, provided enormous margins for the franchisees, provided control for everyone involved and a good retail store became an automated machine after just a few months.

Any product or service offering that requires a monthly fee is an excellent example of automation and control. You sign up a customer once and they become a customer each and every month. Take it a step further and pay your customers to share the product with friends and you've just attained the ultimate form of duplication.

DO MORE WITH LESS

I've told you that one way to increase your knowledge and to be a true power player means keeping abreast of news, trends, and methodologies that can assist your rise to the top. I've emphasized reading as much as you can, whenever you can.

Speed reading has become an almost necessary tool for me in business. Not just because I can whip through articles quicker but it allows me to absorb more information, more information about the industry I'm in and more information about my competition. While the majority of my peers are watching football, I'm ready and researching a variety of different topics, always trying to find an edge.

In addition to an edge on your lazy competitors, you'll be able to:

- Learn languages easier as your comprehension level rises (contrary to popular belief, speed reading actually increases a person's retention)

- Skip over information inside of articles that isn't meaningful and may be repetitive.

Most people read between 100 – 200 words a minute. You must reduce the amount and length of fixations per line to increase your reading speed.

HOW TO SPEED READ

There are several techniques to speed reading but here are the ones I've used. I have increased my reading speed to 400-500 words per minute for moderately complex articles and can finish 250 page books that contain basic ideas in about an hour and a half.

Know your starting point. Like the big red "You Are Here" dot on most maps, you need to know your current reading speed.

To figure out your current reading speed, find a book, any book. This will be your practice book. Your practice book should be about 200 pages and should lay flat when open on a table. Next, count the number of words in five lines. Divide that number of words by five. This is your average number of words-per-line.

Example: 58 words/5 lines = 11.6, which you round to 12 words-per-line

Now, count the number of lines on five pages and divide by five to get the average number of lines per page. Then, multiply this by the average number of words-per-line, and you have arrived at your average number of words a page.

Example: 155 lines/5 pages = 31, 31 lines per page times 12 words-per-line = 372 words per page.

Mark the first line with a pen. With a stopwatch handy, read for 1 minute exactly. Do not read any faster than you normally do. Read for comprehension. When exactly one minute has passed, multiply the number of lines you read by the average words-per-line and you will determine your current words-per-minute (wpm) rate.

Make fewer stops while reading. The fewer times your eye stops in a sentence, the faster you will read. Speed reading is, basically, reducing the number of times the eye needs to stop in order to understand the text being read. There are many methods to speed reading and each one may sound a little different, but, in the end they all work after the same principle: faster reading.

To speed read, you will not be reading in a straight line, but rather in a series of jumping movements. Every jump ends with a "temporary snapshot" of the text that is within your focus area. Each snapshot will last only ¼ to ½ seconds. To understand, close one eye, place your fingertip on top of that eyelid. Then, slowly scan a horizontal line with your other eye. You will feel noticeable movements and times of fixation.

To increase your reading speed, you must eliminate conscious rereading and subconscious rereading by misplacement of fixation. To stop this, you must use conditioning exercises to increase the horizontal peripheral vision span and the number of words registered.

Use a tool. While reading, use a pen, pencil, or your own finger to follow every sentence you're reading. Try to gradually move your hand a little bit faster, noticing your eye's movement. You may notice your eyes following the speed of your hand. Amazing, right?

Using a card, bookmark, or any page-width item could help you increase speed more efficiently, than compared to a pen or pencil. Wider objects cover the rest of the text, preventing your eyes from wandering away.

Holding your tool in your dominant hand, underline each line (with the cap on), keeping your eye above the top of your tool. This serves as a tracker and as a pacer for maintaining steady speed and lessening fixation time. Be sure you hold your tool under your hand, flat against the page.

TECHNIQUE EXERCISE (2 MINUTES):

Practice using your tool as a tracker and pacer. Underline each line, focusing above the tip of the pen. Do not worry about comprehension. Try to keep each line to a maximum of one second, increasing your speed with the following pages. Read, but do NOT take longer than one second per line.

SPEED (3 MINUTES):

Repeat the above exercise, reading each line no longer than ½ second. You may comprehend nothing, which is to be expected. Keep your speed up. Technique will grow as you condition your perceptual reflexes. These exercises are designed to assist the adaptations in your system. Do not decrease your speed. Keep the half a second per line pace. For three minutes, focus above your tool and concentrate on technique with speed. Focus on the exercise, nothing else.

PRIORITIZE CONTENT

Divide the wheat from the chaff: Another primary aspect of speed reading is the idea of prioritizing content. In many books, readers find that there's a lot of "unnecessary information" that can just be skimmed over. In order to find these unnecessary parts, the content will need to be pre-read. This means that the most important parts of the book must be identified by skimming over before you start the actual process of "reading".

It takes practice to be able to distinguish important content from unimportant information. It's critical that you educate yourself at the beginning of a reading session by looking over entire sections of your reading very quickly. Try to recognize patterns of repeated words, concepts, stressed text (bold, italic, and underlined) or other related indicators of important note.

This will help you to "pass over" big portions of the books content, taking time to slow down only when you've come across something you know is important.

How to Calculate Your New WPM Reading Speed

Mark the first line of the selected reading. Read with a stopwatch for one minute, exactly- Read as fast as you can, retaining a comprehension rate. Multiply the number of lines you've read by your previously determined average of words-per-line to determine your new words-per-minute (wpm) rate.

FACING PROBLEMS

If you're having problems with focusing on the reading material, try these tips:

- Have your vision checked. At times, people must read slowly due to an unknown difficulty with their vision. Even if you think that there is nothing wrong with your eyes, have your vision checked.

- Take away distractions: There are a few people who say they read better when music is playing or if they're in a bustling coffee shop. However, if you want to read quicker, you can not permit outside sources to vie for your attention.

- The fewer the distractions, the quicker you will read. Try your very best to find a quiet place to read; make sure the television is off; keep the radio silent. If it's impossible to find a solitary place, use earplugs or white noise headphones to drown out distractions.

- Don't read aloud. Many people tend to sub vocalize or pronounce difficult words under their breath. Some people actually move their lips and others will just repeat words in their head. It doesn't really matter how you sub vocalize—if you do— it will slow your reading down! If you're troubled by this and want to stop this habit, you need to try your hardest to be conscious of it. If you can't stop it by simply being aware of it, then you might want to take bigger and more effective measures. For example, you can put your finger or hand over your mouth while reading. Even though this may seem somewhat extreme, it could be very beneficial in defeating the problem.

Tips to reading faster:

- Read as much as you can. The more you read the more chances you will have to practice reading quicker.

- If you're trying to study and want to use speed reading as a means to do so, do not read three assignments in the time it would take you to read one. Instead, read the same assignment three times for exposure and memory.

- Read as much material as you can with big fonts. It makes it easier to read quicker and helps to avoid skipping lines.

- Fine tune your reading rate to fit the content. Read quicker for simpler content, and slower for content that is more difficult to understand.

- Give reading your undivided attention.

- Remember to keep a tool handy to guide your reading.

- Read in quick quotes rather than separate words. The more often your eye stops during a sentence, the slower you will read, the less you will understand what you read.

- Practice reading with a book that you have previously read. This makes it less complicated to get used to skipping particular words and phrases.

- Pay close attention the first time you read to prevent rereading.

MORE SHORTCUTS TO SUCCESS

- **In a world that is evolving and chang-**ing everyday, the market will reward you for react-ing accordingly. Avoid activities that prohibit your progression including drug use of any kind but especially marijuana. Marijuana dulls the senses, makes you slower and raises your level of apathy, the exact opposite of what you need to succeed as an entrepreneur. All of those "cool" kids that smoke marijuana in high school and college end up to be the losers later on in life.

  - Stop living someone else's dream. You were born with your gut instinct for a reason. Advice from others is often times only a reflection of what they would have wanted for themselves, not what's best for you. Remember this the next time someone ask you for advice, they are looking for guidance in realizing their dreams, not yours.

  - Placebos are underrated and probably more powerful than you realize.

- One of the most powerful character assets you can develop is the ability to work through problems.

- Bad things do happen to good people.

- In any business, you are going to have clients and customers. Be sure that you are always capturing their contact information. You'll need to communicate with them later, believe me. Do this by using email service blasts, text messaging blasts, social media and blogs. If you need an example, send a text message from your mobile phone with the word Andrew (no periods (.) or punctuation marks) to phone number 313131. You can also see how my blog is set up at www.andrewrinehart.us/blog

- Protect your ideas and designs with trademarks and patents. The world is evolving quickly to an online world and that isn't going to change any time soon. Thinking of names for your new business? Always check with your state offices to see if the entity name is available, and then check with the United States Trademark Office (www.uspto.gov) to see if the name has already been trademarked and lastly, check the domain name availability with a company like www.godaddy.com.

- You are not a product of your upbringing. You can change anything and custom design your life in to anything you want.

- Hard work will take you further than intelligence.

- Golfer? Distance and accuracy don't come from upper or lower body strength; they come from coil and tension. Specifically the upper body coiling up against the lower body, creating tension; much like a wound up spring. Remember to "GASP" before every swing, that is, take a deep breath and focus on Grip, Alignment, Stance and Posture. A lot of the same principles apply to the game of tennis as well.

- Have a conflict or hurt feelings with a person? Go talk with them in person about it, the old fashioned way.

- Eating two Honey Crisp apples each day (one in the morning and one in the late afternoon) will help eliminate skin blemishes, acne, cold sores, diarrhea, stomach cramping, constipation and low energy. I've been doing it for years and I rarely miss a day without my honey crisp apples.

- Go in to debt for items that appreciate. Pay cash for items that depreciate.

- Donate blood often. It has been said that one of the reasons women live longer than men is because they menstruate every month, getting rid of toxins in the body and bloodstream.

- Remember the top five regrets by those dying (as researched by a nurse after asking patients for thirty years).

  1. I wish I'd had the courage to live a truer life to myself, not the life others expected of me.

  2. I wish I didn't work so hard.

  3. I wish I'd had the courage to express my feelings better.

  4. I wish I had stayed in touch with my friends more.

  5. I wish that I had let myself be happier.

- Notice that the previous bullet point mentioned not having enough "courage" twice.

- Perception is, in most cases, reality.

- Last but not least, always remember that you are more powerful than you realize.